KNOW
THE**GAME**

uk:athletics

# Athletics

Produced in collaboration
with UK Athletics

Produced for A & C Black by

Monkey Puzzle Media Ltd
Gissings Farm, Fressingfield
Suffolk IP21 5SH

Published in 2006 by

A & C Black Publishers Ltd
38 Soho Square, London W1D 3HB
www.acblack.com

First edition 2006

Acknowledgements
Cover and inside design by James Winrow for
Monkey Puzzle Media Ltd.
Photographs on page 7 courtesy of Adidas. Front
cover and photographs on pages 5, 6 (top), 12, 13, 17
and 43 courtesy of Empics. Photograph on page 25
courtesy of Getty Images. All other photographs
courtesy of UK Athletics' official photographer
Mark Shearman.
Illustrations by Tim Bairstow of Taurus Graphics
and Dave Saunders.

KNOW THE GAME is a registered trademark.

Printed and bound in China by C&C Offset Printing Co.,

Note: Throughout the book players and officials are
referred to as 'he'. This should, of course, be taken to
mean 'he or she' where applicable.

# CONTENTS

# STARTING OUT

**A**thletics has been a popular activity since long before the first Ancient Olympic Games in 776BC. Indeed some events – such as sprinting, endurance running, javelin and discus – have changed very little since those first contests.

Modern techniques in training mean that today's athletes are fitter than ever before, and some of the current records would have been unimaginable even 10 years ago.

## GET INVOLVED – FIND A CLUB

If you would like to get involved in athletics, you need to find your local athletics club. There are approximately 1,500 clubs in the UK, welcoming all ages and athletics activities. To find out more about your local athletics club go to www.ukathletics.net.

## THE TRACK

Modern tracks have two parallel 'straights' joined by two semi-circular bends. They are 400m around, measured at a distance of 30cm from the inside edge, or 'kerb'. Tracks are divided into six to ten individual lanes, each 1.22–1.25m wide. Lanes are numbered from inside to outside: lane 1 is closest to the inside.

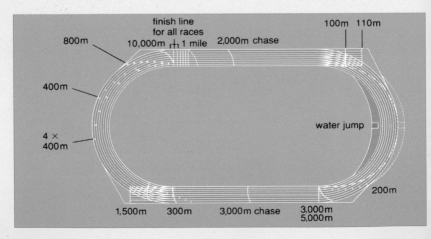

Sprint races (distances up to and including 400m) are run in these separate lanes throughout. 800m races use the lanes as far as the end of the first bend; 4 x 400m relay uses them for one complete lap plus the first bend of the second lap.

## The start

In races using lanes and involving a bend, runners in outer lanes start further ahead. The effect is that they run the same distance as those inside them. Races from 1,500m upwards are not run in lanes, so a curved start line is used.

## The finish line

The finish line is always at the end of the 'home straight'. It is marked by a line drawn at right angles to the inside edge of the track where the straight joins the bend.

## The field

The area in the centre of an athletics facility is used for 'field athletics' such as hammer, javelin or high jump. Long jump and triple jump take place off to the side of the track, often right in front of the spectators, which can make these very exciting competitions to watch or take part in.

Lane numbers are clearly marked at the finish line.

**National performance targets**

**These appear throughout the book and are a guide to the national level standards for each track and field event in the UK.**

# EQUIPMENT

**M**ost stadium equipment is provided by the stadium. It includes photo-finish equipment, electronic timing displays, stands for judges and timekeepers, lap indicator boards, bells, water jumps, steeplechase barriers, hurdles and starting blocks.

### Hurdles

Hurdles are height adjustable, from 1.067m down to at least 0.762m. Adjustable counterweights are attached to the base so that, whatever the height, it will take a force of at least 3.6kg to overturn the hurdle.

### Starting blocks

Starting blocks are required to be rigid and fasten to the track so as to cause the minimum damage to its surface but, this aside, they can be any design or construction provided they don't give an unfair advantage. Owners of synthetic tracks can insist on their own blocks being used.

 The hurdles in use.

### Clothing

Clothing must be non-transparent, even when wet, and designed and worn so as not to cause offence. The usual competition wear is an athletics vest and shorts. Athletes will wear club colours when competing for their club.

**Some athletes have their own starting blocks.**

Standard adjustable starting blocks.

## Shoes

Shoes are highly specialised for different athletics competitions. For runners, ridges, grooves or other indentations are allowed on the sole and heel, provided they are of the same basic material as the sole. Each shoe may also have up to 11 spikes. On synthetic surfaces these may not exceed 9mm; on non-synthetic surfaces up to 25mm is allowed. The maximum diameter of each spike is set at 4mm.

Generally, distance runners use shoes with more cushioning and less grip, while sprinters go for the lightest possible weight and more grip.

Shoes for field athletics are even more specialised than running shoes. There are different kinds available for each of the jumping events, javelin, and throwing events.

Sprint shoes

Endurance shoes

High-jump shoes

Triple-jump shoes

Javelin shoes

## IDENTIFICATION

Competitors are required to wear identification numbers on their chest and back, so that officials can identify them and record their results.

In running events with photo-finish equipment, the organisers can also ask athletes to wear additional numbers stuck to the side of their shorts or their legs. This is so that they can be identified in a photo of a close finish.

# WARM-UP AND COOL-DOWN

## WARMING UP

Warm-up is necessary before commencing vigorous activity. Its purpose is to raise the internal temperature of the body and make the tissues surrounding joints more pliable. Warming up properly gives you:

- greater range of movement, and so more effective application of force
- less chance of injury.

Warming up should take up the first 20 to 40 minutes of a training session. It should begin with 5 to 10 minutes of gentle exercise such as jogging. It's best to do this on a soft surface such as a grass infield, rather than the cinder or synthetic surface of a track.

This gradual beginning should lead into 10 to 15 minutes of stretching exercises in which all joint complexes should be progressively exercised to their outer limits of movement. It is important to pay particular attention to those parts of the body that are going to have to work the hardest in the training or competition to follow. It is also important to bear in mind that such a session is an integral part of the warm-up. Specialised training is also needed away from the warm-up – e.g. in the cool-down or as a seperate session – to improve all round flexibility.

## COOLING DOWN

Cooling down after competition and training is an equally important activity. Its purpose is to reduce body temperature and pulse rate slowly so that blood flow through the muscles remains relatively high and the waste products resulting from exercise are removed. In this way post-exercise stiffness and soreness are reduced. It need not take so long as warm-up, nor be so complex; five to 15 minutes of easy jogging, walking and stretching will usually suffice.

### STRETCHING SENSATION

During cool-down or during a stretching session never stretch any muscle until it is painful. Stretch until you feel a little tension, then take a few deep breaths and relax into the stretch a little more. Finally come out of the stretch as you breathe out one of the deep breaths.

Some examples of exercises that can be used as part of your cool down or training to improve flexibility.

groin

hamstrings

triceps

obliques

chest

quadriceps

upper back

hip flexors

outer thigh

calf

9

# THE SPRINTS

**S**prints are the most high profile and glamorous events in track and field athletics. The 100 metres final is traditionally the blue-ribbon event of the Olympic Games.

## THE 100 METRES AND THE 60 METRES

The 100 metres is the standard short sprint competition distance; the 60 metres is its indoor equivalent. The race can be broken down into three parts:

- the start, which is followed by rapid acceleration (or 'pick up') for 40–60m (in the 100m)
- beyond 60m, speed decreases, which the athlete attempts to minimise by relaxing
- finish – dip for the line.

### Starting

For international contests, starting blocks and a 'crouch start' are used. The starting commands for all races up to and including the 400 metres are: 'On your marks' and 'Set'. When all are steady in the set position, the gun is fired.
The basic form of the crouch start is generally referred to as the 'medium' start:

- front foot 35–45cm behind the start line
- rear foot 35–45cm behind the front foot

- in the set position, the angle behind the front knee should be 90 degrees
- in the set position, the rear leg should be slightly flexed
- the rear block face should be set at a steeper angle than the front one.

### STARTING TIPS

- Raise your hips to just above shoulder height on the command 'Set'.
- Do not let your shoulders move in advance of your hands and let your weight act mainly through your front foot.
- Move gradually into an upright position as you run from the blocks.

## The middle of the race

During pick-up, in which great acceleration takes place, work hard against the ground in the initial stages, changing to lighter, more agile movements as top speed is reached. Speed is maintained by running 'tall' (keeping the hips and chest high) with a high knee-lift and 'clawing' foot contacts (pulling the foot backwards), which pull the athlete along each time the foot strikes the ground.

## Finishing

Towards the end of the race, the 'lift' is achieved by making the running action lighter and quicker. The 'dip' finish, in which the athlete thrusts their torso forwards at the line, is often mistimed: it loses its value if begun before the final stride to the line.

### National performance targets (in seconds) – 100 metres

|        | Seniors | U-20  | U-17  | U-15  |
|--------|---------|-------|-------|-------|
| Male   | 10.40   | 10.75 | 11.00 | 11.50 |
| Female | 11.80   | 12.10 | 12.30 | 12.50 |

Colin Jackson coaches the basic starting position.

USA's Lauren Williams wins a close 100m final at the World Championships in Helsinki.

## THE 200 METRES

While 200 metre sprinters, are almost as quick as their 100 metre counterparts, they must also be able to maintain high speeds over longer distances. They also have the added technical difficulty of running the first half of their race while going round a bend at high speed. The 200 metres race begins at the bend diagonally opposite the finish line. All the runners stay in their starting lane until the finish, so the starts are staggered so that the distance to the finish is the same for each competitor. On a standard track, lane 2's start line is 3.51m in advance of that of lane 1, and subsequent start lines are 3.83m in advance of each inside adjacent one.

It is usually advantageous to run close to the left-hand lane line, but don't forget that you can be disqualified for running on or across the line.

### Starting

Because the start takes place on a curve, there are two extra starting principles, in addition to those of the 100 metres start (see pages 10 and 11):

- the starting blocks are positioned to the outside of the lane, facing slightly inwards towards the visible crown of the left-hand lane line
- the left hand is placed roughly 5cm behind the start line, so that the runner's shoulders are square-on to the direction he or she is going to run, and at right angles to their spine.

The bend can make it hard to work out who is ahead, until the runners hit the straight!

The pick-up should not be quite so forceful as that for the 100 metres, because the 200 metres is run with more control. The first 100 metres should be run 0.2 to 0.4 seconds slower than the sprinter's best 100 metres. Around the curve, athletes need to lean slightly inwards and press their left shoulder forwards a little, to increase efficiency.

**Bend into straight**

The most difficult part of the race is where the bend joins the straight. Top speed has been reached and the accumulated centripetal forces of the bend are at their greatest. Continuation of the bend techniques, coupled with relaxed, light, high-cadence running will resolve the difficulties adequately. Speed decreases nearer the end of the race than in the 100 metres, so 200 metres specialists have a slightly heavier training load, over longer distances (200/300/400m).

## National performance targets (in seconds) – 200 metres

|        | Seniors | U-20  | U-17  | U-15  |
|--------|---------|-------|-------|-------|
| Male   | 21.20   | 22.00 | 22.50 | 23.50 |
| Female | 24.10   | 24.90 | 25.30 | 26.00 |

200-metres races often have extremely close finishes.

# THE 400 METRES

The 400 metres race represents sprinting at the limit of a sprinter's lactic anaerobic energy supply system. This effectively means that it's the longest distance in which a runner can go at or near his or her full speed. Go this fast for the next distance up, the 800 metres, and your muscles would stop working properly long before the finish!

### The stagger

The 400 metres lasts for one complete lap of a standard 400-metre-long track. For the runner in lane 1, the event begins at the finish line: because two bends are used, the staggered starts necessary from lane 2 outwards are quite considerable. Lane 2 is 7.04m in advance of lane 1, and then lanes further out are 7.67m in advance of their adjacent inside lane.

### Speed v. lactic acid

To race 400 metres successfully, you need to be able to balance speed against the build-up of lactic acid in your muscles. Your race strategy has to be aimed at arriving at the finish line just as the amount of lactic acid in your muscles has reached a point where it affects your speed. An important part of a 400 metres racer's training is to build up a resistance in their body to lactic acid build-up. If this is achieved, a sprinter's 400m time should be roughly twice their best 200 metre time, plus 3 or 4 seconds.

> As in the 200 metres, be careful not to step on or cross the inside lane line, or you will be disqualified.

### Stages of a 400 metres race

- The first 100 metres

  The pick-up phase will not be as accentuated as that of the 100 or 200 metres. Full speed need not be reached until the early part of the second 100m.

- The middle 200 metres

  The middle of the race should be given over to running at the target pace, with a long, controlled stride. This pace should be sustained into the second bend, but more effort will be needed to maintain it as the bend unwinds. If the first half of the race is run too fast, this middle phase may end with the sprinter struggling.

- The last 100 metres

  The last 80m is always an effort to keep a controlled stride against the 'tying up' effect of increasing fatigue.

| National performance targets (in seconds) – 400 metres | | | | |
|---|---|---|---|---|
| | Seniors | U-20 | U-17 | U-15 |
| Male | 47.10 | 48.80 | 50.50 | 53.50 |
| Female | 54.50 | 57.00 | – | – |

Note: female U-17 athletes run 300m in competition

Tim Benjamin wins a tight finish in the 400 metres at Crystal Palace.

## THE 4 X 100 METRES RELAY

The 4 x 100 metres relay involves four sprinters combining forces to move a 50g baton around one lap of the track. The baton is 28–30cm in length and 12–13cm in circumference.

### Changeover zones

The baton is passed from one sprinter to another within a 20m-long changeover zone straddling each 100m section of the race; these zones are marked with yellow lines. Each changeover zone is preceded by a 10m-long pre-changeover zone, marked by an orange line, within which the outgoing runner can stand. However, the baton must not be exchanged in this area.

### Lane position

Legs 1 and 3 involve running a bend, so common sense dictates that those runners run close to the left-hand lane line, in the same way as 200 metres runners. Runners 2 and 4 must therefore run in a line that takes them on the right-hand side of their lane, so that the incoming runner doesn't run into them. Because of this, the incoming runner carries the baton in their right hand and the outgoing runner receives it in the left.

### Passing the baton

The baton is passed using either a 'down pass' or 'up pass'. Properly executed, the down-pass is quicker, since it permits about a metre of 'free distance' between each athlete. The up-pass is safer

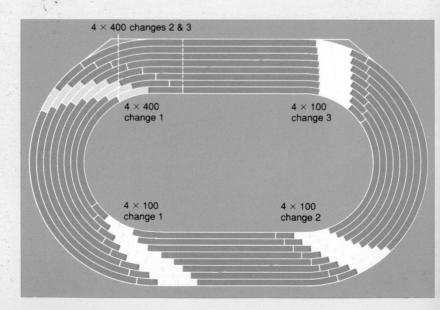

4 × 400 changes 2 & 3

4 × 400 change 1

4 × 100 change 3

4 × 100 change 1

4 × 100 change 2

because it is easier to rescue if the timing of the changeover goes wrong.

One disadvantage of the up-pass is that it requires runner 1 to grasp the first quarter of the baton; runner 2 then takes hold of the second quarter, runner 3 the third quarter, and runner 4 the final quarter. Because the baton is only 30cm long, any error can mean that there is not enough room on the baton for runner 4's hand. Batons are often dropped in such circumstances.

## KEY POINTS

The incoming runner:

- runs flat out until after the baton has been passed on
- calls 'Hand' or 'Stick' when close enough to exchange the baton
- places the baton firmly into the receiver's hand.

The outgoing runner:

- presents a steady hand on the call, keeping it steady until the baton is passed.

### Check marks

Runners must practise changes and work out 'check marks'. These are placed on the track at a point in front of where the incoming runner reaches the beginning of the acceleration zone. The outgoing runner starts as the incomer passes the mark, accelerates flat out, but is still caught by the incoming runner in the final third of the changeover zone. Check marks are approximately 5.5m from the beginning of the acceleration zone for inexperienced athletes, and 7.3–7.9m for club runners, and are placed at the side of the lane.

Baton changeover in a 4 x 100 metres relay race. This 'down pass' is harder to get right, but also faster than an 'up pass'.

## THE 4 X 400 METRES RELAY

The 4 x 400 metres relay involves four runners combining to move the baton around four laps of the track, each running one lap in the process.

### Use of lanes

The first 500m of the race is run in lanes; thus the starts are staggered even more than those for individual 400m races. Runner 1 races the whole 400m in his or her lane; runner 2 races the first 100m in lane, then is allowed to cut across to the inside kerb of the track. The point at which runner 2 is allowed to leave his or her lane and cut to the track kerb is identical to that used by 800m runners, and is marked by a green line across the track.

There is no acceleration zone for the 4 x 400m changeovers. The international colour code for the changeover areas is blue, and the start lines have a blue bar at their centre.

### Changeovers

Since the incoming runner is very tired, the exchange needs to be visual, with the outgoing runner looking back as they collect the baton (unlike that of the 4 x 100 metres). The outgoing runner judges when to start running, taking the baton in their left hand as they move away from the zone. This permits the incoming runner to remain on the left-hand side of

### POSITIONING AT CHANGEOVER

Runners 3 and 4 take up their positions at the beginning of the changeover zone according to the position in which their incoming runner is lying, i.e. second from the kerb if lying second, third if lying third, etc. This is straightforward when positions are clearly defined but, in practice, last-minute changes of running position frequently occur. As a result, the changeovers can become quite combative, with pushing and shoving as runners try to make sure they have the best position possible.

the lane, while the outgoing runner occupies the right-hand side. This positioning provides some shield against collisions with other runners.

The incoming runner must present the baton from the right of the incoming athlete, so the baton has to be changed from left to right hand at some time during the run. The best time to do this is immediately after clearing the changeover zone. (Don't change hands in the changeover zone itself, as the risk of it being knocked from your hand is too great.)

Katherine Merry takes up the baton for Britain in the 4 x 400 metres relay.

**Collecting the baton safely is mainly the responsibility of the outgoing runner.**

# THE 110 METRES (MEN) AND 100 METRES (WOMEN) HURDLES

Sprint hurdles is a speed event, so a good hurdler has similar training to a sprinter. That said, many elements of the event are a compromise for a sprinter:

- the 'wrong' foot may have to be further forward in the blocks (to reach the first hurdle taking off on the 'correct' foot)

- during the pick-up, the athlete has only seven or eight strides in order to come upright

- there is a barrier clearance every fourth stride.

On the other hand, certain elements of sprinting have to be exaggerated:

- run 'tall' so that the hurdle can be attacked better

- incline forwards in order to aid dynamism across each hurdle

- be 'active' coming off the hurdle

- maintain high hips through the landing

- concentrate on quick arm actions between barriers (quick arms promote quick legs and fast running).

## HURDLE HEIGHT

Adult men race over 110m, women over 100m. There are also different versions for children.

|  | Hurdles | Height |
|---|---|---|
| **Men** | 10 | 106.7cm |
| **Women** | 10 | 84.0cm |

| National performance targets (in seconds) – 100/110 metres hurdles | | |
|---|---|---|
|  | **Seniors** | **U-20** |
| **Male** | 14.50 | 15.60 |
| **Female** | 14.10 | 15.00 |

Note: U-17 athletes compete over shorter distances.

Clearing a hurdle: the lower height of women's hurdles means they are more upright across the hurdle than men.

## THE 400 METRES HURDLES

In this event, men and women run one circuit of the track, in lanes, hurdling barriers of 91.4cm and 76.2cm in height respectively. The first hurdle is spaced 45m from the start and subsequent hurdles at 35m intervals.

It takes between 20 and 24 strides to reach the first take-off. After this, there is a rough link of –6 or –7 to the number of strides between the hurdles. So, a 20-stride approach leads to 13 or 14 between hurdles, 21 to 14 or 15, and so on.

The use of an even number of strides over the early barriers is rare since it requires the ability to hurdle equally well off either leg, and most hurdlers have a preference for one leg or the other.

At hurdles 5 or 6, the onset of fatigue will bring about an increase in the number of strides between barriers. Whether this progresses through one additional stride for two barriers, then to two strides, depends on the athlete's ability to hurdle from either leg. The more gradual the change, the better.

| National performance targets (in seconds) – 400 metres hurdles | | |
|---|---|---|
| | **Seniors** | **U-20** |
| **Male** | 52.00 | 55.30 |
| **Female** | 60.20 | 64.50 |

**It is safest to lead into the hurdle with your left leg: leading with the right can cause disqualification if you trail your inner leg around the barrier.**

The 400 metres hurdles is one of the most draining events in athletics, combining hurdling and speed endurance.

## DISTANCE EVENTS

**D**istance events cover a wide range of types of running. The 800 metres is becoming close to a sprint as athletes get ever fitter. At the other end of the spectrum, the 10,000 metres and marathon are almost entirely endurance based.

### THE 800 METRES

The 800 metres is run in lanes as far as the end of the first bend, so the starts are staggered by roughly the same amount as for the 200 metres. (The actual formula for calculating and measuring the distance is in the IAAF Handbook.) The 800m start line is identified by a green centre bar. The 'break line' (the point at which the athletes can leave their lanes and run to the inside lane) is at the junction of the first bend and the back straight, and is also coloured green.

### Tactics

A planned, even use of energy and distribution of effort is ideal. However, tactics may demand that athletes run at a fast pace in order to 'burn off' known 'kickers' (athletes with a strong sprint finish), or at a more conservative pace in order to permit oneself to 'kick' at the finish.

### TRAINING AIMS

The 800 metres taxes the aerobic/anaerobic energy systems in the ratio of approximately 65:35. For the 1,500 metres it is 50:50.

- Develop a well-balanced running posture and springy running action.
- Build up aerobic endurance and work capacity.
- Train the anaerobic energy system in order to develop and combine endurance with speed.
- Develop power (especially in the legs) and general strength endurance.

| National performance targets (in minutes/seconds) – 800 metres | | | | |
|---|---|---|---|---|
| | **Seniors** | **U-20** | **U-17** | **U-15** |
| **Male** | 1:48.5 | 1:52.5 | 1:57.5 | 2:05.0 |
| **Female** | 2:06.0 | 2:12.0 | 2:15.0 | 2:18.0 |

## THE 1,500 METRES

The 1,500 metres event, also known as the 'metric mile', is three-and-three-quarter laps of the track. Runners start from a white line that curves across the lanes just before the end of the first bend. The athletes line up in a set order, and as soon as the gun goes they can cut across to the inside lane, as long as they don't hinder an opponent.

### Tactics

Running to a planned energy utilisation and effort distribution is at least as important as it is in the 800 metres. Running next to the kerb helps to achieve this, but do not become 'boxed in' by other competitors so that you cannot get out to overtake. Running wider than the outside of the second lane, particularly around bends, increases the distance and wastes energy.

| National performance targets (in minutes/seconds) – 1,500 metres | | | | |
|---|---|---|---|---|
| | Seniors | U-20 | U-17 | U-15 |
| Male | 3:42 | 3:53 | 4:04 | 4:18 |
| Female | 4:20 | 4:36 | 4:40 | 4:48 |

The starting command for distance races is 'On your marks', followed by the gun being fired once everyone is ready. There is no 'Set' command.

Double Olympic gold medallist Kelly Holmes in action.

## THE 5,000 METRES

The 5,000 metres starts from a curved white line situated at the beginning of the second bend. It is run over a distance of 12.5 laps. Before 1995, women ran 3,000 metres instead, but they now compete over the same distance as men.

The aerobic/anaerobic requirement for the 5,000 metres is in a ratio of roughly 80:20. There are often mid-race surges in speed, as runners try to shake off weaker opponents. This means that 5,000-metre runners need to have endurance speed plus the ability to change pace.

5,000-metre runners also need strong resistance to lactic acid build-up. This can be achieved in training by running for longer than 40 seconds, at faster than racing speed, with short breaks of 2 to 4 minutes. Training sessions like these should cover between 3km and 4km in total.

### FARTLEK TRAINING

Fartlek or mixed-pace training incorporates changes of pace into a continuous run. These pace surges can be pre-planned and controlled, or allowed to evolve naturally depending on how the athlete feels.

| National performance targets (in minutes/seconds) – 5,000 metres | | |
|---|---|---|
| | Seniors | U-20 |
| Male | 13:50 | 15:30 |
| Female | 16:30 | 17:30 |

Putting in a surge of speed in the middle of the race can sometimes shake off one or two people from the leading group.

# THE 10,000 METRES

The 10,000 metres, also known as the '10K', is the longer of the two long distance track events run at major championships. The race starts at the start/finish point, from a curved white start line, and covers through 25 laps of the track. The distance is very draining, therefore athletes do not race this distance as often as shorter events.

The 10K's aerobic/anaerobic ratio requirement is approximately 85:15. Although the training is very similar to that of the 5,000 metres, running for over 30 minutes requires an increased level of endurance capacity.

Oxygen consumption during a 10K race is in the region of 180 litres, and this suggests that the quantity of training should increase by some 30 per cent compared to the 5,000 metres. The bulk of the extra distance should be run at a continuous, fast pace.

| National performance targets (in minutes/seconds) – 10,000 metres | |
|---|---|
| | **Seniors** |
| **Male** | 29:10 |
| **Female** | 35:30 |

Even after 25 laps of the track, and numerous changes of pace, the 10K sometimes comes down to a sprint finish, as here at the World Championships in Helsinki.

## THE MARATHON

Although the marathon is held on roads, since its instigation as part of the modern Olympic Games, in 1896, it has been held as part of the track and field competitions within the summer games. At major championships the marathon usually starts and finishes in the main athletics stadium.

The event, steeped in ancient myth, has the ethos of struggle over adversity and this is carried to each event by all modern-day competitors. To most competitors the challenge of completing the distance is the major objective. The distance is sufficient to prove a challenge to all who start and that challenge has made the event the most popular of participated in athletic events throughout the world.

### Training for the marathon

Modern experience has shown that 'athletes', having undergone widely different preparations, complete the distance. The preparation will be dictated by a number of factors including starting fitness, time available and commitment.

Often the amount of work required will be given in terms of the number of miles covered in each week. This may vary from a small amount to over 100. The make-up of the miles run should vary from short runs to long runs and the pace should vary from below expected race pace on the long ones to faster than race pace on the shorter runs. Runs of varying pace should also be included and all of the combinations will give variety which makes the training more enjoyable.

If you are considering running a marathon try to plan as far in advance as possible. Rome wasn't built in a day and neither are marathon runners.

### Hitting the wall

This is the term commonly used to describe that time in a marathon when a feeling of exhaustion sets in due to the body having used those energy stores readily available from within. This can start to take place between 32–34 km. From there on, pace deteriorates and it can be a struggle to get to the finish line.

### GOING THE EXTRA MILE (AND A QUARTER)!

Until 1908, marathon courses were approximately 40km in length. At the London Olympic Games of that year, the course was lengthened to 26 miles 385 yards so that it could start on the Royal lawns of Windsor Castle and finish in front of the Royal box at the stadium. The race has been run over this same distance ever since, 42.195km.

One of the main factors in avoiding this situation is pace judgment. Too fast early in the race can mean depletion of energy stores earlier than if a pace based on a realistic finishing time is followed.

## KEEP HYDRATED

Part of making the experience of running a marathon as comfortable as possible is to ensure that the body is well hydrated before the start but (don't over do it) and that liquids are taken on board throughout the race. This will ensure that overheating due to lack of fluid does not become a problem. This can be further assisted by taking advantage of sponges at sponging stations and therefore cool the skin surface.

Marathon running has become popular with leisure runners who relish a challenge, as well as being a highly competitive event.

Paula Radcliffe, who in 2002 set a women's world marathon record of 2:17.18.

## THE STEEPLECHASE

The steeplechase is run over 2,000m and 3,000m, though only the 3,000m is raced at major championships. Barrier heights are 91.4cm for men, 76.2cm for women.

- The 3,000m takes place over seven laps plus part of a lap, the 2,000m over five laps plus part of a lap.
- The laps may be 390m or 410m long, depending on whether the water jump is inside or outside the second bend; the former is more common.
- The 3,000m start is positioned either halfway down the back straight or two-thirds of the way around the second bend.
- The 2,000m start is positioned halfway down the home straight. It is not possible to run the shorter event with an outside water jump.

### The barriers

There are four barriers plus a water jump. These are 79m or 82m apart. The first barrier is not introduced until over 200m has been run, and the water jump is not crossed until after the first portable barrier has been cleared. All barriers are solid enough for the athlete to be able to jump on and off with safety.

▶ The water jump is the most tiring obstacle in the steeplechase, and requires a special technique.

### THE WATER JUMP

The water jump technique involves stepping on to the barrier, then pushing hard with the supporting leg to project over the water. If successful, the runners land far enough out of the water, on the other leg, that they can step out on the subsequent stride. Tips include:

- keep your hips low and your supporting leg bent while on the barrier rail
- delay the push off until the body weight has passed beyond the barrier, and then to push back against the barrier, in order to maximise the drive.

## Training and techniques

The steeplechase demands the abilities of a fast middle-distance runner coupled with sufficient strength and agility to clear the barriers. Steeplechasers need first to be effective between barriers, and must train as mid-range runners (see pages 22–25). Steeplechasers must also be competent hurdlers. Efficient hurdlers are able to save energy and time that will prove invaluable later in the race. Good steeplechasers learn to hurdle from both legs.

This is important because the barrier is often sighted through a crowd of other runners, who make it difficult to judge distances and to adjust stride patterns in the approach.

| National performance targets (in minutes/seconds) – steeplechase | | |
|---|---|---|
| | **Seniors** | **U20** |
| **Male (3,000m)** | 8:50 | 9:30 |
| **Female (3,000m)** | 10:25 | 11:00 |

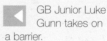
GB Junior Luke Gunn takes on a barrier.

# TRACK EVENT TRAINING

**T**raining should be planned ahead, working back from the date of the competition. For an elite athlete of some years' experience, the starting point will be at least 12 months. For a complete beginner, the minimum time needed to get a reasonable standard of fitness is about 24 weeks.

Most coaches divide the annual training plan into three distinct blocks of training, often referred to as 'macrocycles', which have recuperation, preparation and adjustment, and competition as their successive individual aims.

## TRAINING PHASES AND RECOVERY

### Recuperation phase

This is a period of active recovery from the training and competition stresses of the previous year, evaluation of the past year, and planning for the year to come.

### Preparation phase

Lasting until the beginning of the next competitive season – usually some six months – the 'preparation phase' is sub-divided into two phases:

- gradual improvement of the aerobic base, general strength, local muscular endurance, mobility, and technique development
- training for the specific needs of competing in a particular event.

During its earliest weeks, the phase concentrates on the heightening of the levels of speed/anaerobic/strength endurance and absolute strength (where necessary), coupled with continued technique development. In the final weeks, this phase emphasises speed, speed endurance and elastic strength, while continuing strength endurance and technical development.

Distance runners often find running off-road useful, as the softer ground is less harsh on their joints and muscles.

> Recovery is just as important as the training itself. Without recovery your body doesn't get full benefit from training.

Junior female athletes complete technical hurdles drills in preparation for the steeplechase.

## Competition phase

The 'competition phase' is characterised by a general reduction in training quantity, though not quality, in order to maximise energy and focus on the achievement of competitive goals. For those in the shorter running events, in which a number of peaks are possible during the season, it may be prudent to return to a period of hard training during the mid-cycle phase so as to be able to attain higher levels of performance during the final weeks, or even just to maintain form. This is not possible in those longer events in which recovery times between peaks of effort are more extended.

### OVERTRAINING

Too much training without enough recovery is a recipe for disaster. Here are some tips:

- have a hard day followed by an easier day
- have no more than three working days in succession
- two recovery days in every fortnight
- one easy week in every month.

These tips make sure that an athlete's body is not excessively worked, and must be included in the overall training plan.

## TRAINING TO IMPROVE ENERGY SYSTEMS

Training aims to improve the systems of energy supply for activity in two areas:

*Immediate short-term energy supply*, or anaerobic mechanism, which requires no oxygen to work. This has two sub-divisions:

- alactic anaerobic energy is very short-lived (no longer than about 10 seconds) and produces no lactate as a by-product
- lactic anaerobic energy lasts up to about 40 seconds and produces carbon dioxide, water and lactic acid as by-products.

*Long-term energy supply* (the aerobic (or 02) mechanism), which requires oxygen in order to operate.

There are three main systems for running training:

- continuous
- intermittent, and
- Fartlek (see page 24).

### Continuous training

A run of a single duration is completed at a fixed pace. It has two sub-divisions:

- steady runs of medium pace carried out close to the anaerobic threshold over distances of 4km to 10km. A rough-and-ready guide to this pace is that you cease to be able to converse easily while running
- steady runs of slow pace but long duration (30 minutes or more), conducted at pulse rates between the anaerobic threshold and its aerobic equivalent, which can be

Cross country forms an important part of most endurance athletes' winter programme, to develop strength and the aerobic system.

roughly calculated using the formula 70 per cent of 220 minus your age. These runs provide the main endurance base for the longer events in particular.

The aerobic effect of this type of training is long term.

## Intermittent training

This type of training involves several runs separated with periods of rest. The rests may be either active or passive. There are two types:

*Interval training*, which develops the aerobic side of endurance, and which is further divided into:

(i) short distances of between 200m and 400m in length, with rests of between 30 seconds and 3 minutes, or

(ii) longer distances of over 800m, with recovery periods of between 1 and 5 minutes.

The aerobic effect of this type of training tends to be short term.

*Repetition training*, which works on the anaerobic side of endurance, and which has three sub-divisions:

(i) speed training, conducted over very short distances in order to develop sheer speed. Recoveries here need to be somewhere in the region of 4 to 6 minutes

(ii) short distance/short recovery training over distances up to 400m, in which the recovery time should roughly equal that of the run. It, in turn, can be separated into:

(a) strength endurance, in which quality is sacrificed by keeping rigidly to recovery times so that the session rapidly hurts

(b) speed endurance, in which individual runs are grouped in sets, with a longer recovery span between each set, in order to maintain quality over more runs

(iii) long duration/long recovery training over distances from 300m to 1000m, in which recovery may last up to 10 minutes in order to keep work output at its highest. Speed runners will work over shorter distances than endurance runners.

Speed is the essence of this work. Runs need to be made at greater than 80 per cent of the best performance for the distance.

 Warm-up drills for middle-distance athletes.

# JUMPING EVENTS

The field events within track and field athletics includes jumping events and throwing events. The jumping events include the high jump, long jump, triple jump and pole vault.

## THE HIGH JUMP

High jumpers may use any technique they wish with the aim of jumping the greatest height possible. Most use the 'Fosbury Flop' style, in which the approach run is curved through its final four strides. This curve induces rotation about the vertical axis once jumpers leave the ground, causing them to pass over the bar and land on their back.

### Take-off technique

'Flop' approach runs are capable of being longer and faster than those of other styles – 8 to 12 running strides, as opposed to six to eight.

- Take off from the foot furthest from the bar. In essence the 'flop' is a scissor-jump, executed from a curved approach and utilising a back lay-out.

- Make the free leg action a bent one (see the third element of the figure below).

- Avoid initiating rotation about the vertical axis to present the back to the bar using body movements. This rotation should come from forces stored during the final curve of the approach run.

This 'Fosbury Flop' technique was named after Dick Fosbury, the American who invented it in 1967.

**Double-footed take-offs are forbidden.**

## In the air and landing

In flight, the jumper should adopt a loose backward arch, with head and heels pulled in (see the fifth element below), and avoid the temptation to look at the bar. Clearance of the feet and lower leg is effected by a delicately timed straightening, the product of repeated practice. The landing should be made on the upper back and shoulders.

## Alternative styles

Until the advent of the 'flop', the straddle-jump was the dominant style. A tiny number of athletes still use it. It has a straight approach, and the jumper takes off from the foot closer to the bar. In flight, jumpers rotate, belly down, about the bar, to land on their back. Where the jump has to be executed into a sandpit, rather than a foam landing bed, the only safe form of jump is the 'scissor', in which the landing is made on the feet.

### SECOND ATTEMPTS

Jumpers are allowed to abort the jump before take-off and repeat it, provided that this all takes place within a 60-second time limit. They may not 'break' the vertical plane between the uprights and then re-take, however.

**During competition the bar is generally raised by 5cm, 3cm or 2cm increments.**

| National performance targets – high jump | | | | |
|---|---|---|---|---|
| | Seniors | U-20 | U-17 | U-15 |
| Male | 2.10m | 2.00m | 1.90m | 1.80m |
| Female | 1.78m | 1.72m | 1.68m | 1.60m |

## THE LONG JUMP

Long jumping looks deceptively simple. In fact, the technique and timing of a long jump are tricky to get right, and there are several different styles of jump to try before you find the one that suits you best.

### The approach run

Speed built up during the approach run is what gives the jump distance. The approach run has three distinct phases:

- a beginning, characterised by rapid acceleration and a forward inclination of the jumper

- a mid-phase, during which speed reaches a high level and the jumper attains an upright carriage

- a conclusion, characterised by maintained posture as leg speed reaches a crescendo, bringing horizontal speed to its peak.

Good quality jumpers will need runs of between 18 and 22 running strides long, with the quickest runners using the longest runs. For younger athletes, a rough guide is 12 strides for 12-year-olds, 14 strides for 14-year-olds and 16 strides for 16-year-olds.

### Take-off

Take-off is characterised by the maintenance of a high hip position and vigorous vertical actions by the free leg and the opposing arm. The foot plant should be flat-footed rather than heel first.

### RUNWAY MARKERS

The rules say that markers to show where to start your run-up may not be placed on the runway. However, most top-flight jumpers get around this by placing markers just off the runway to the side, allowing them to judge exactly where their run-up should begin.

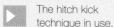
The hitch kick technique in use.

## Long jump styles

The simple, natural style of long jumping, in which the knees are tucked up to the chest is known as the 'sail'. The sail is very inefficient. Much more distance can be gained using other styles.

- The 'hang' style

  In this, both legs are allowed to trail behind the body in flight, before being brought forwards for landing.

- The 'hitch kick'

  In this, the legs continue in a running action in flight – 1 rotation for normal long jumpers and 2 for the best.

- The stride jump

  The modern trend is towards keeping the leading leg and take-off leg separated for as long as possible, in a simple, stable flight position before landing.

> The distance is measured to the part of the mark in the sand that is nearest the take-off board.

The 'stride' style of long jumping comes from the Eastern European school of jumping and is an effective technique to learn. During mid-flight the thighs are held apart for as long as possible.

## National performance targets (in minutes/seconds) – long jump

|  | Seniors | U-20 | U-17 | U-15 |
|---|---|---|---|---|
| Male | 7.40m | 6.90m | 6.60m | 6.00m |
| Female | 6.00m | 5.70m | 5.50m | 5.25m |

## THE TRIPLE JUMP

Triple jump consists of a hop, a step and a jump, made in that order. This demands that the hop landing is made from the foot from which the jumper took off. The step landing is thus made on the opposite foot to that from which the hop take-off and landing was made. Under current rules, touching the ground with the 'free' leg during the jump is no longer considered an offence.

This event is really a very simple one. In its modern form it has no clearly defined contrasting styles. Technique tips include:

- the vast majority of jumpers keep the hop low in order to conserve horizontal velocity and attempt to achieve an approximately even balance between the length of each phase of the jump
- most jumpers also change their arm action from the alternating one of the approach run to a simultaneous one through each landing and take-off.

### Successful triple jumping

In addition to natural and trained springiness and resilience, the keys to success lie in:

- controlling speed and body position through the initial take-off
- maintaining an erect body position in flight
- achieving an active, 'pawing' leg action through hop and step landings.

### Rules

Competition facilities are identical to those of the long jump, except that the take-off board has to be placed far enough away from the pit for the hop and the step landings to be completed before it is reached. A distance of 21m from the far end of the pit is prescribed; one of 13m from the near edge is recommended for men's international competition. For younger and less able jumpers it is usual to place the take-off board 9–11m from the near edge of the pit.

The triple jumper takes off more horizontally than the long jumper, and makes active, clutching strikes at the ground as he maintains an upright torso.

### Women's triple jump

The women's event is now well established and a fully integrated competition programme has been successfully adopted into mainline athletics. Women take off from an 11m board, and for junior competition a 9m board may be located on the adjacent long jump runway. However, this is quite unsuitable for club standard participation.

> #### HIP POSITION
>
> Triple jumpers make their initial take-off with their hips further forwards than long jumpers. Triple jump approach runs are similar in construction to those of long jump (see page 36) but are generally not so fast.

Great Britain's Nathan Douglas takes to the air.

| National performance targets – triple jump | | | | |
|---|---|---|---|---|
| | **Seniors** | **U-20** | **U-17** | **U-15** |
| **Male** | 15.50m | 14.00m | 13.50m | 12.50m |
| **Female** | 11.80m | 10.30m | 9.80m | 8.80m |

## THE POLE VAULT

The pole vault is one of the most spectacular field events, with the best competitors soaring to amazing heights. It always draws a lot of interest during big international events. Women's vaulting is now established alongside men's as an important part of the competition scene.

> **Vaulters are allowed 2 minutes to complete their jump.**

### Technique

Most vaulters make their vault approach run using an even number of running strides. This is enables the vaulter to hold the pole comfortably at the start of the run.

Right-handed vaulters will grip the pole with their right hand nearer the top, carry it on their right-hand side and take off from their left foot. Left-handers will operate vice versa. The vaulter's take-off foot should be directly under his top hand at the moment he leaves the ground.

Staying back away from the pole is critical to the proper execution of the early swing phase of the vault. That achieved, the hips must swing rapidly overhead before the pole reaches the vertical if the fly-away is to project vertically rather than laterally.

▶ Energy is stored in the pole during the plant, take-off and hang phases; the hips must be overhead before that energy straightens the pole. The vaulter's strength and momentum then drive him up off the pole, and hopefully over the bar.

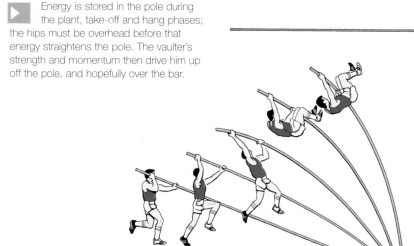

## Pole grades

Modern poles are graded according to the load that will bend them, applied at a particular height. Thus a 14/150 pole will bend in response to a 150 lb (68kg) load being applied at 14 ft (4.3m) from its base. Such a pole would be suitable initially for a 68kg vaulter gripping at 4.3m from the base with his top hand. They are thus highly personalised items of equipment and vaulters are permitted to use their own in competition, which are unavailable to other competitors.

There is no restriction on the size or weight of the pole. The surface must be smooth, although a binding of no more than two layers of adhesive tape is permitted in order to improve grip.

### NOT ALLOWED

- Vaulters may not go above the grip taken by their upper hand after take-off. In effect this prevents any form of climbing the pole.
- It is not allowed to replace the bar with your hands, having knocked it off with your body.

| National performance targets – pole vault | | | | |
| --- | --- | --- | --- | --- |
| | Seniors | U-20 | U-17 | U-15 |
| Male | 4.80m | 4.30m | 4.00m | 3.00m |
| Female | 3.35m | 3.10m | 2.80m | 2.30m |

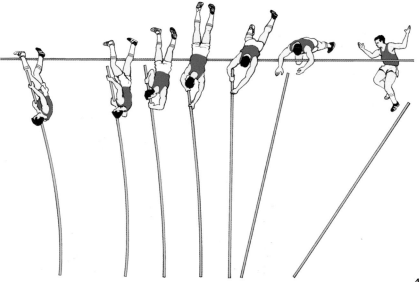

# THROWING EVENTS

The throwing events are shot put, hammer, discus and javelin. These are among the oldest athletics events – the trials of strength and technique involved in throwing a long distance have been part of sports contests for thousands of years. Today, each of the throwing events is open to both men and women.

## GENERAL THROWING RULES

Competitors taking part in throwing events are required to:

- start the throw from a stationary position

- land the implement completely within the inner edges of the lines marking the landing sector, which for shot put, discus and hammer encloses a segment of 40 degrees (the landing sector for javelin is approximately 29 degrees), and retire from the delivery area (circle or runway) only after the implement has landed

- in retiring, step first on to the ground outside the circle behind the line separating front and back halves, or behind the extended delivery arc (javelin).

When throwing from a circle, competitors are not permitted to make contact during the course of a throw with either the top of the circle rim, the stop board or the ground outside the circle. The same principle is applied to the javelin in relation to the scratch line and runway boundaries.

### Unfair advantage

Limitations are placed on the use of devices or special taping that give one competitor an unfair advantage over the others, although competitors are permitted to give protection to bona fide injuries and to use substances on their hands

If an implement breaks during the course of a throw, competitors are given a further attempt even if they lost balance as a result and contravened other relevant rules.

in order to improve their grip. Only hammer throwers are permitted to wear a protective glove. Spreading substances on the surface of the circle or runway is not allowed.

### Own equipment

Competitors are allowed to use their own implements rather than those of the organisers, but these must be checked and approved beforehand, and may be used by other competitors once permission has been given from the implement's owner to do so.
At major championships the organisers provide all implements new from the manufacturers.

## MEASURING THROWS

Distances are measured from the mark made by the implement on landing, or the place where the judge saw it land, whichever is nearer to the delivery area (to the inner edge of the circle rim or javelin delivery arc/scratch line). All throws are now measured to the nearest centimetre, odd or even, below the actual reading on the tape or shown on the automatic measuring device.

Vera Popisilova-Cechlova of the Czech Republic in the women's discus final at the World Championships in Helsinki.

## THE SHOT PUT

There are two major styles of modern shot putting – the linear technique and the rotational technique.

> The shot must be held in one hand, at the shoulder and close to the chin, without moving behind the line of the shoulders during the course of the throw.

### Linear technique

Athletes adopt a back-facing starting stance at the back of the circle, supported mainly on their right leg (if they are right-handed).

- The shot is given initial momentum by making a small hop towards the front of the circle, bringing athlete and shot into a side-on delivery stance.

- Next the legs, torso and finally the arms apply force in a sequential action as the torso twists towards the front. The shot is released from a high position above the stop board.

▼ In the 'linear' style, athletes hop to the delivery position from the rear of the circle and thrusts the shot into orbit using their legs more than their arms.

## Rotational technique

The 'rotational' or 'spin' style has been around since the late 1960s. The rotational style of throwing remains popular in the USA but has also become popular in Europe. The split between 'linear' and 'rotational' styles at major games is now slightly in favour of the rotational technique and championships are now being won by the 'spinners', although it continues to be more unreliable than the 'linear' style of putting.

The style is essentially a modification of a discus throw (see page 48), in which athletes make a running rotation around their left foot (for a right-hander), going from the back of the circle to the front in the process. Because the circle is smaller than a discus circle, the action must be tighter and more controlled. The delivery position at the front half of the circle is on a narrower base for similar reasons. From such a position it is possible to achieve a strong lift from both legs.

Centrifugal force causes the shot to tend to come away from the neck; the athlete must press the shot hard against the neck right through to the end of the movement.

### National performance targets – shot put

|        | Seniors         | U-20          | U-17          | U-15             |
|--------|-----------------|---------------|---------------|------------------|
| Male   | 16.00m (7.26kg) | 13.20m (6kg)  | 14.50m (5kg)  | 13.00m (4kg)     |
| Female | 13.50m (4kg)    | 12.00m (4kg)  | 10.80m (4kg)  | 10.50m (3.25kg)  |

In the rotational style, athletes make a running rotation around their left foot (for a right-hander), going from the back of the circle to the front in the process.

## THE HAMMER

The hammer event takes place from a circle identical to that for the shot put, except that it has no stop board. Like the discus, the implement is thrown from within the confines of a safety cage.

The hammer throw is made at the end of a series of spins of increasing speed. The implement is given initial movement with several swings, before the thrower begins to spin about their left foot (for right-handed throwers). After three or four spins the movement is suddenly stopped: the hammer is heaved and released high over the thrower's left side.

### Pre-spin technique

Initially, a rear-facing stance is adopted with the upper body turned very slightly to the right and the hammer behind to the thrower's right side. The hammer is then lifted and swung anti-clockwise up and across the body.

Throughout the whole of these actions the left shoulder should not move backwards. As the implement swings up, the arms bend to allow the hands to pass close to the thrower's forehead. The arms then extend again as the hammerhead falls back to its low point to the right of the thrower.

▼ The three standard turns of the hammer throw which follow the preliminary swings, viewed from the landing area. Note how the thrower works under and ahead of the hammer as it moves through its high point.

## Into the spins

Usually two or three swings are sufficient for the thrower to feel ready to enter into the spins. Thereafter, the thrower moves with the implement, pivoting firstly on the heel of the left foot and then completing on the ball of the foot. The right foot leaves the ground and moves with the thrower during the second half of the turn when pivoting on the ball of the left foot. There are two distinct styles of working thereafter. In the first of these, three such turns are completed. In the other, four turns are involved, but the first of these must be made entirely on the toe of the left foot in order that the whole sequence can be accommodated within the confines of the circle.

### HAMMER RULES

- At the start of the throw, the head of the hammer may be placed on the ground outside or inside the circle.
- There is no penalty for the implement striking the ground during the course of the throw.
- The thrower may wear gloves.
- Hammer throwers may stop their effort and start again within the 60-second time limit (as other throwers are permitted to do), except when they have stopped specifically as the result of the hammer striking the ground.
- If the hammer strikes the ground, throwers can stop and compose themselves while keeping the implement moving by passing it from hand to hand around them.

Britain's Shirley Webb at the World Championships in Helsinki.

| National performance targets – hammer | | | | |
| --- | --- | --- | --- | --- |
| | **Seniors** | **U-20** | **U-17** | **U-15** |
| **Male** | 58.00m (7.26kg) | 45.00m (6kg) | 50.00m (5kg) | 43.00m (4kg) |
| **Female** | 50.00m (4kg) | 45.00m (4kg) | 40.00m (4kg) | 35.00m (3kg) |

## THE DISCUS

### Technique

Discus throwers adopt a back-facing straddle stance at the rear of the circle before they begin their throw.

- Movement starts with one or more easy rhythmic swings of the discus around and across the body.

- Next comes a turning run around the left foot (for a right-handed thrower).

- Rotation about the vertical axis continues when the thrower's right foot is placed at the centre of the circle, and until the left foot, having left its position at the back, eventually comes to ground at the front.

- Rotation is brought to a halt by vigorously stopping the left side, causing the discus-carrying right arm to flail laterally.

**Good balance is crucial for a discus thrower.**

Basic discus technique is shown in these diagrams. Like the shot putter, the discus thrower starts facing away from the landing area and makes a turning rotation around his feet before slinging the discus.

## Varieties of technique

Discus has less varied techniques than shot or hammer – all throws are basically rotational – but there are one or two minor sub-styles within the general rotational concept of the event.

Two technique differences relate to the manner of moving away from the back of the circle to its centre: A wide swinging action of the right leg, which is then rapidly folded as it comes to its position at the centre of the circle. Some throwers also make the initial turn on the heel of their left foot, transferring on to the toe before it leaves the ground. These throwers have to be very skilled if good balance is to be retained.

Making the initial turn entirely on the ball of the left foot, keeping the swinging right leg closer to the central turning axis.

Further stylistic differences relate to what occurs at the front of the circle at the moment of delivery. One school adheres to a 'fixed feet' style of throwing, keeping both feet in contact with the ground at release. The other concentrates on driving vertically through both legs, causing loss of ground contact.

Discus throwers are allowed to use chalk to improve their grip on the discus. They may not wear gloves.

### DISCUS SIZES

The full-size discus is 22cm in diameter and 2kg in weight for men, and 18cm and 1kg for women. Smaller discs are available for younger throwers with smaller hands to use, with the size and weight depending on their likely hand size and strength.

## National performance targets – discus

|  | Seniors | U-20 | U-17 | U-15 |
|---|---|---|---|---|
| Male | 50.00m (2kg) | 40.00m (1.75kg) | 43.00m (1.5kg) | 38.00m (1.25kg) |
| Female | 45.00m (1kg) | 41.00m (1kg) | 37.00m (1kg) | 30.00m (1kg) |

# THE JAVELIN

Javelin is not divided into clear technique groupings like some of the other throwing disciplines. Even so, the subtleties of technique swing between two variations:

- a linear carry in which power is directed along the line of the javelin

- a more rotational technique in which the thrower's non-throwing side turns away from the direction of the throw, with the throwing hand following the movement. The best exponent of the rotational style is the current world record holder Jan Zelezny, who has thrown 98.44m.

### 'Pulling' technique

Javelin is essentially a 'pulling' event. The javelin must be held ready behind the thrower's body and pulled forwards.

- The throw begins with an approach run, during which the javelin is carried over the shoulder of the throwing arm, which gives initial horizontal momentum. The final actions should not detract from this or negate it, but should enable the velocity to be increased smoothly.

- The javelin is moved backwards ('withdrawn') at the point where the approach run blends into the delivery itself. This normally starts as a right-handed thrower's left foot moves forwards on the fifth stride from delivery, and is completed during the subsequent two strides.

- The penultimate stride ('the impulse stride'), has to be the best stride of the run-up. To achieve this the thrower must actively run off the non-throwing-side foot and move the throwing-side foot forwards and downwards. This encourages an effective

The final three cross-over strides, following a running carry of six or more strides, bring the javelin thrower sideways-on and enable the legs to be used ahead of the arm in much the same way as in the shot and discus.

hip strike position, putting the body in a position to perform a chain of movements from the ground through to final foot strike and then release. The torso does not lean back; the throwing arm does not lower – some of the cardinal sins of the event involve misunderstanding of these two points, plus the tendency to 'stroke' back the right foot before it makes contact with the ground.

- In the final stride the front leg is braced against the forward and rotational thrust of the rear leg, which brings the hips and torso forwards, ahead of the arm. The arm flails into action, elbow leading, both late and fast.

### ESSENTIAL JAVELIN RULES

- The javelin must be held at the grip.
- It must be thrown over the shoulder or upper part of the throwing arm.
- It must not be slung or hurled.
- At no time during the throw may competitors turn completely round so that their back is towards the throwing arc/scratch line.
- Non-orthodox throws are not permitted.

## National performance targets – javelin

|        | Seniors        | U-20           | U-17           | U-15            |
|--------|----------------|----------------|----------------|-----------------|
| Male   | 69.00m (800g)  | 57.00m (800g)  | 55.00m (700g)  | 48.00m (600g)   |
| Female | 46.00m (600g)  | 43.00m (600g)  | 37.00m (600g)  | 33.50m (600g)   |

# COMBINED EVENTS

**T**he combined events embrace the decathlon and its female equivalent, the heptathlon. Each represents an extension of the all-rounder principle that influenced the development of the pentathlon (involving long jump, discus, javelin, sprint and wrestling) in the Ancient Olympics.

Modern combined events feature ten events in decathlon and seven events in heptathlon. Because of the number of events, the competitions take two days each to complete. This, as much as anything else, sets participants apart from other athletes.

▼ The world's best heptathletes compete over hurdles at the World Championships in Helsinki.

### Scoring

Points are awarded to competitors for their best performance in each event of the competition. The number of points they get are taken from a scale prepared by the International Amateur Athletic Federation and published in a booklet called *Scoring Tables for Men's and Women's Combined Events Competitions*. The book is revised periodically, taking into

account general progress in each event and the advancement of the world record. The nearer to the current world record competitors get, the more points they earn. The athlete gaining the greatest

points total over all events is the winner. Ties are resolved by awarding the higher placing firstly to the competitor who achieved the higher score or placement in most events; then, if still unresolved, to the athlete who attained the highest single-event score.

## Rules

Generally speaking the rules of each individual event are applied, except in the following particular instances:

- athletes are permitted one more false start (three as opposed to two) before being disqualified for starting infringements in running events

- only three trials are permitted in long jump, shot put, discus and javelin.

### Failing to score

Failure to record a performance in an event, such as registering three no jumps in long jump, merely reduces the total potential score by that amount. Failure to participate in an event at all brings about elimination from the overall competition.

### DECATHLON EVENTS

The individual elements of the decathlon in competition order are as follws.

- First day – 100 metres, long jump, shot put, high jump and 400 metres
- Second day – 110 metres hurdles, discus, pole vault, javelin and 1,500 metres.

### HEPTATHLON EVENTS

Heptathlon competitions are run in the following order:

- First day – 100 metres hurdles, high jump, shot put and 200 metres
- Second day – long jump, javelin and 800 metres.

## National performance targets – combined events

|        | Seniors   | U-20      | U-17        | U-15        |
|--------|-----------|-----------|-------------|-------------|
| Male   | 6,500 pts | 5,000 pts | 4,300 pts[1] | 2,300 pts[2] |
| Female | 4,800 pts | 4,100 pts | 3,900 pts   | 2,600 pts[2] |

Notes [1] Scores in octathlon (8 events) using appropriate UK age group implements.
[2] Scores in pentathlon using appropriate UK age group implements.

# FIELD EVENT TRAINING

Field eventers, particularly the throwers, are power athletes. Their forte is speed and strength coupled, which form the basics of their training. The general information about training on pages 30 and 31 will also be useful to field atheletes.

## SPEED

All field event athletes require an element of speed for their event. Running activities that develop pure speed, speed endurance and strength endurance will predominate, particularly during the second phase of preparation and into competition. Speed can be improved using:

- repetition runs made over distances from 30m to 80m, repeated four to six times, with full recovery intervals
- acceleration runs in which speed is built to a crescendo.

The latter can be practised usefully on jumps runways, where the rhythms can be made to approximate those of the jump's approach run itself. Such short, fast running is also very important to throwers.

Speed endurance can be improved by any of the following three means:

- flat out repetition runs made over slightly longer distances than used for speed development, e.g. 80–150m, allowing a full recovery between each
- running at 90% effort over slightly shorter distances, e.g. 60–120m, with 30–60 seconds rest between runs and 10 to 15 minutes between sets
- 'ins and outs', in which distances of between 60m and 150m are divided into three sections run fast/slower/fast, for six to eight repetitions run in one or two sets, with a full recovery between each run and a longer one between sets.

## STRENGTH

Strength endurance can be improved by:

- hill and sand-hill repetition runs made up 80–150m inclines of less than 10 per cent, during which care must be taken to keep good posture and good running form
- 'turnabouts' or 'back-to-backs', run over 30–100m with 20–30 seconds recovery between runs and 2 to 5 minutes between each of two sets of four runs

- resistance runs, made over very short distances in which a tyre, weighted sled or resisting partner is towed.

It is also possible to develop strength endurance by means of circuit training or stage training (a refinement of circuit training in which all of the sets of each exercise are completed before moving on to the next), using either callisthenic exercises employing body weight, stacked weights such as multi-gyms, or barbells and dumb-bells.

Strength can be divided into 'gross' or 'elastic' strength.

- High levels of elastic strength are vital to jumpers and throwers. Improvement can be achieved by working a light resistance rapidly, or through plyometric exercises in which limbs absorb force before expressing it, as when catching and throwing medicine balls or when jumping down and rebounding.

- Gross or maximum strength is expressed in lifting the heaviest possible weight once. It is necessary to improve gross strength in order to be able to improve other facets of strength. Equally, the advancement of gross strength is in turn dependent on improvement of all-round general strength. All are inter-connected and cannot be developed fully in isolation.

Some training exercises for throwers with a medicine ball.

# COMMON FAULTS – FIELD EVENTS

**T**his section aims to give advice about faults that athletes commonly develop in their field event techniques. However, it is no substitute for working with a properly qualified UKA coach.

## THROWING EVENTS

### Shot put/discus/javelin

**1) Landing in the pre-delivery position with body weight off the rear foot**
Correct this by practising to land with the body weight acting firmly through the rear foot, or with the chin and right knee over it in the case of the shot put and discus.

**2) Inability to keep the right hip ahead of the implement**
This can be caused by allowing the hip to go 'soft' (move backwards) on landing, or by beginning the delivery with the arm and shoulders, rather than with the legs. Correct it by keeping the right hip pressed forwards on landing, and by using the hip and legs in preference to the arm and shoulders. Throwing events are leg events.

**3) Failure to offset the front foot**
Correct this fault by repeated practice, concentrating on getting the foot into the correct position.

**4) Front foot offset too far to the left**
This is generally caused by late placement of the foot. Correct this by tidying and quickening the footwork. (In discus, the tidying action is very important.) Compensate by trying to place the foot to the right of the line of throw.

▶ The shot put requires huge strength and skill – as demonstrated by Britain's Carl Myerscough.

## 5) Inactive rear leg/hip at the start of the throwing action

With the shot put and the discus, ensure that the landing is on the ball of the foot; then twist the foot and right hip actively in the direction of the throw. When throwing the javelin, the foot faces at 45 degrees to the direction of the throw, and the outer heel can be pushed out, or the right knee turned in, to create the same effect.

## 6) Failure to brace the left side against the throwing action

This can be corrected by keeping the left shoulder high and the chest up through the throw, and by seeking muscular tension all down the left side of the body.

### Shot put

## 1) Lifting the head and torso during the early stages of the shift

This can be corrected by thinking of staying low. Ask someone to hold their hand at the required height and work to stay under it. Delay the right leg thrust slightly so that it drives you towards the front of the circle instead of upwards.

## 2) Failure to turn the right foot approximately 60 degrees towards the direction of the put

Correct this by practising the shift without the shot, and concentrate on turning the right foot into the required position.

## 3) Dropping the elbow of the active arm during the putting action

This is corrected by consciously keeping the elbow high, at shoulder level, during the putting action.

### Discus

## 1) Imbalance

This is generally most apparent at the front of the circle, but it has its origins at the rear. Lack of accuracy here will be magnified as the turn progresses. Centre the body weight firmly over the left foot at the start of the turn.

## 2) Using the left shoulder to initiate the turn

Keep the shoulders passive while turning through the legs and feet.

## 3) Allowing the throwing arm to drop close to the right hip at the end of the turn

Correct this by keeping the hand high, and/or keeping space between the discus and the body.

> **Balance is the key to the rotation-based throwing events.**

## Javelin

### 1) Withdrawal made too late in approach run

Restructure the approach so that at least four strides remain after withdrawal has commenced.

### 2) Poor final alignment of javelin

The javelin must be aimed just below the intended flight path. The commonest causes of poor alignment are:

- dropping the throwing arm
- dropping the throwing hand (i.e. a loose wrist)
- loosening the grip of the fingers, or any combination of these
- losing body position prior to release.

Correct these faults by concentrating hard on the particular problem area.

### 3) The arm is used too soon

Wait for the front foot to land before bringing the arm into play.

### 4) A low throwing elbow

This is a dangerous fault because it can lead to elbow injury. Correct it by concentrating on keeping the throwing hand high, and turn the throwing hand medially and upwards prior to release.

Steve Backley – Great Britain's most successful male javelin thrower.

## Hammer

### 1) Incorrect hammerhead path during the swings

Adjust the hammer's low point until it is just off the right toe, or by adjust the high point until it is just behind the left shoulder.

> **The runway approach of the javelin shares the same principles as horizontal jump events.**

## 2) Poorly balanced entry to the turns

Body weight should act centrally, or slightly left of centre. Correct this fault by working to achieve this.

## 3) 'Pulling' or leading the turn with the left shoulder

This can be corrected by delaying the entry a little until the hammer has passed the mid-line, and by working strongly through the legs.

## 4) Imprecise footwork during turning

The foot action is complex; it takes time and repeated practice to master. The left foot must be a clear heel-toe action; unless the heel turn progresses through a full 180 degrees, the thrower will move across the circle and not down it.

## 5) Shortening the hammer's radius by bending the arms

This occurs when more centrifugal force than the thrower can handle is generated. Correct it by slowing down slightly, and by concentrating hard on remaining relaxed so that the arms extend towards the hammerhead, letting it 'find its own path'.

Lorraine Shaw of Great Britain in action at the European Cup.

## JUMPING EVENTS

### Approach runs

**1) Inaccurate take-off**
Usually caused by running too fast, or by overstriding through the early and middle sections.
Check that the correct foot has been placed on the start mark.

**2) Poor running (hips low, bad balance)**
Concentrate on keeping hips high, running 'tall', and running lightly. Body weight should be slightly forward so that ground contact is made through the ball of the foot.

**3) Unequal distribution of effort**
All approaches have three running phases: acceleration, consolidation (or body alignment) and quickening (or attack). Straining or working too hard through the early and middle phases is a common mistake; failing to quicken the stride rate through the final phase is another.

### Take-offs

**1) Forcing the take-off by lowering the hips**
Forget trying to jump upwards. Concentrate on keeping the hips high, and simply running 'off the ground'.

**2) Inactive free leg**
Emphasise the upward punch of the free leg to hip height. Hold it there.

**3) Poor use of arms**
Vigorous use of the arms will aid the jump. Arms are used

simultaneously in the high jump, and the step and jump phases of the triple jump, but in opposition (one forward, one back) in the long jump and triple jump hop take-offs.

**4) Poor body position**
Keep the head up, the chest out and the back erect and in tension throughout the take-off.

### High jump

**1) Landing too near the edge of the landing bed**
Take-off position is too near the centre of the uprights. Adjust the approach run accordingly.

**2) Hitting the bar on the way up**
Caused either by leaning towards the bed and anticipating the 'lay-out', or by taking off too close to the bed. To correct this, lean out towards the centre of the approach curve, or move the start mark and thus the take-off position further out from the bed.

**3) Hitting the bar coming down**
Caused by the flight parabola being too far forwards. Correct this by adjusting the start mark so that the take-off is moved closer to the bar and bed.

### Long jump

**1) Dropping the free leg too soon**
This is a common weakness of the 'hang' style in particular. Correct by concentrating on keeping the free knee high for longer.

## 2) Forward rotation in flight

This is caused by poor body alignment either at take-off or in flight, or both. In order to correct it, keep the head up and/or the chest out, and keep the torso erect.

## 3) Sitting back in the sand on landing

This is caused by leaning back in flight, or attempting to get the feet too far forwards. Attempt to do the opposite in either case.

## Triple jump

### 1) Poor jump rhythms (e.g. big hop, short step)

Correct this by:

- curtailing the hop and emphasising the step by holding the leading knee higher

- listening to footfall rhythm and making adjustments of emphasis

- placing guidance markers alongside the runway and working to them.

### 2) Hop is too high

This is a common fault. Drive forwards instead of upwards, in order to carry runway speed into subsequent phases.

### 3) Inactive landings

Work to pull the landing foot under you, against the ground, in a 'clawing' action on hop and step landings.

## Pole vault

### 1) Lack of pole control during the approach run

Learn to use the arms as shock absorbers to keep the pole steady during the run.

### 2) Late 'plant'

This is a common fault for beginners. Become positive in pushing the pole out towards the box in good time. Try placing a cue mark alongside the runway if you can't manage otherwise.

### 3) Off-line 'plant'

Being off-line to the vaulter's right is more common than to the left. This is generally caused by a late 'plant'. Correct this by planting early and getting the right hand overhead by the time the tip of the pole enters the box.

### 4) Tucking or inverting too early

Delay the action by permitting the take-off leg to trail slightly, or by maintaining an extended body position.

### 5) Insufficient inversion

The tuck and swing forwards should be tight and quick. The top arm should stay extended, and the hips should end up high overhead. Practise on a gym climbing rope and through 'pop-up' drills, in which an inverted position is held until landing, from a short approach run.

# INDEX